Creative W
Plot Engine

Ganga Bharani

http://gangabharani.com/

About The Author

Ganga Bharani Vasudevan is the author of 'Just you, me and a secret', 60 Creative Writing Prompts and Plots book 1 and book 2, and Plot Engine, among others.

Her short films 'Tiny Steps' and 'Candles' won the Best Film Award and Special Mention Award in an international film festival. She was awarded 'Best Urban Chennai Blogger Award'.

She is now writing a script for an Indian Feature film that will be released in the year 2017.

She works with an MNC as a Robotics Engineer, too.

Learn more about Ganga at https://www.amazon.com/Ganga-Bharani-Vasudevan/e/B008G99BKM/

Website: http://gangabharani.com/

Books By Ganga Bharani Vasudevan

Just you, me and a secret

Plot Engine

Creative Writing Prompts and Plots Book 1

Creative Writing Plots Book 2

A Minute To Death

A Sip of Love and a Sip of Coffee

Plot Coaching

       I am starting my plot-coaching program very soon. In this course, I will help aspiring authors find plots and assist them with developing these plots into interesting stories. This is not grammar coaching or writing-style coaching. In this program, we'll focus on the story. My creative writing prompts and plots books will give you an idea of what you can expect from this program. Contact me at gangabhraniv@gmail.com for an introductory session.

Introduction

Every story is a collection of words put together in the right order with a hand full of punctuations here and there. When it's a love story there can only be two people falling in love, either happily end the book or make it a tragedy. But then how can each story be different from the other? It's the characters, setting, plot and the order of happenings that make one story different from the other. That makes every one of you develop a plot into a story that's entirely different from the other.

For example if we are talking about a love story with a man and a woman falling in love it sounds like only two variations are possible using this prompt- happy ending and tragic ending. Let's say 100 people in a room are use the same prompt to develop their story. Choosing one of the two variations you are already different from 50 writers in the room.

What if you make the woman a doctor and the man an engineer? At least 50% of others, who use your prompt won't think of the same combination. So 75 people are writing something else.

Now, let's say your story is happening in India. 20% of the remaining will not be writing about India or any country you choose. So 20 of you are writing almost the same story as of now.

You now add a few more characters, incidents and dialogues. You also add a suspense to the story. Do you think anyone else will be writing the same? Not at all. No two people can write the same prompt the same way.

This book will provide you with a list of creative plots, each of which can be twisted and turned into several stories. This book will serve as a story guide.

As writers, we all want to tell stories and keep the readers engaged. In this book, you will find 80 prompts. This is not like the other prompt books that you find in the market where they just list one-liners as prompts. In this book, you will be given prompts or plots and ways to develop them into various genres. These prompts will not just create a spark in you to create your own story but also guide you to twist and turn them into a story you will be comfortable writing.

Let's not waste too much time reading the introduction. Let's get straight into the prompt section.

Plots:

1. Plot:
You are driving on, a lonely road. The street lights are dull. The street is too quiet. When you drive down, you see someone throwing away a huge black plastic bag on the street and flying away instantly. You slow down to see what's thrown. You notice the black cover moving. You get curious, you stop the

car and get down to see what's in there. You open the bag to see,

Development

a.   A spirit comes out of the bag. (Makes it horror)

b.   A puppy is in the bag. Finding the culprit and the reason behind him throwing away his dog. (Makes it a nice social drama. A good lead for a short story, maybe)

c.   A broom marked as a gift addressed to you. (can make it a fantasy like harry potter)

d.   A man almost dying can make you develop it into a crime thriller. Who put him there? Who is he? Why was he beaten so badly? What's his back story?

2. **Plot:**
Walking in a park, you see an old couple talk. Suddenly, the old man falls to the ground, unconsciously.

Development

a.   This can be developed into a romance novel. Telling the couple's back story. Tragic or happily ever after depends on what you want to write and how you write it.

b.   You can make the man fall after a gunshot making it a thriller. Why was he shot? Who is the woman next to him? Who shot him?

i.   This can again branch out into a family drama kind of crime where the sons shoot him for the property.

ii.   Making him a politician can turn your story into a political drama.

iii.   Random shot in a shootout. So what's the back story of those shooters? Why were they in the park? Or what's the back story of the old couple and how it met with a tragic end.

3. Plot:

A guy is selling toys in a market and he has been doing that for years. One car stops in front of his shop and a lady gets down from it. She walks straight to his shop and hands over some money.

Development

a.   There can be a back story where the girl visits the shop as a child, had no money to afford the toy and this guy, who was also young at that time, gives a toy for free. She is here to repay. A good scope for a love story between a super model and a poor guy.

b.   One side love story in which this guy, not so good looking and not so rich, falls for the rich and glamorous girl. He is being ignored and finally they fall in love.

c.   She might have hired this guy for murdering someone related to her business. You can make her a business woman.

d.   This guy can be an undercover cop and her, a colleague. They might be on an undercover operation and the currency she handed to him was a kind of clue or a code communication.

4. **Plot:**

A girl stands at the top of a building. He looks at her from several floors below, from the ground. A minute later she jumps.

Development

a. A suicide. Why did she commit suicide? How is she related to him? Maybe he was here to stop her from jumping and it became too late.

b. Revenge. He was waiting for her to jump. Maybe he drugged her, made her stand at the top of the building, where no one noticed him and quickly descended down the stairs to join the crowd later. Waits for her to jump watches her die. Why did he do that?

i. Giving a reason that attributes to personal revenge.

ii. She was a journalist and had solid evidence against him, a business man or a politician. This can widen the scope of the story.

iii. You can make it a film shooting. Where she jumps but then lands on several cushions lined up on the floor. This could open up to a love story between an actress and him, a common man.

5. **Plot:**

He opens his laptop in the middle of the night. He receives an email from a girl. It reads that she died two days ago and also explains how she died.

Development

a. She is a known girl, someone he is emotionally bound to. This will make him find the killer and take revenge.

b. She is someone unknown. This will scare him. This story can be twisted into a horror story where the girl haunts him, makes him punish her killer and then leaves him alone.

c. Making him a journalist and her an actress can develop into a mystery ride. She wanted to send it to him before she dies so that he finds her killer.

6. Plot:

Out of nowhere, someone breaks open into your house and points a gun at your head.

Development

a. Burglars. Theft. Maybe even some love and sympathy in the story.

b. Terrorist. Hostages. Politics into the story.

c. Narrowing the roles of burglars, what happens to the family after most of their possessions are robbed? This can develop into a family drama involving poverty, family values, love and family bond.

7. Plot:

You are stuck in an elevator that stops midway. The power goes off. There is a handsome guy beside you.

Development

a. You can turn it into erotica.

b. You can make them fall in love making it romance.

c. You can make it horror by making one of them as a ghost. There can be a backstory for this ghost in the lift. You can stir the scary pot by making the guy get out at a floor that's not even part of the building and later when he comes out he can find that the lift was not functional for months together. He can then come back to find who the girl was.

d. You can make the girl murder the man. Maybe this is a story of revenge and cutting the power in the building was a part of her plan.

8. Plot:

You are blindfolded and dragged into a van. You are taken for a half an hour drive. Then, you are pushed out on the ground and you heard the van drive away. You remove the knot around your hand with so much effort and remove the cloth tied around your eyes. You run around to find that you are stuck in a maze.

Development

a. This can be developed into something like Maze Runner.

b. You can make it a reality show.

c.   You can make this a dream and start off with how a person's real life is like a maze.

d.   Or this could be a romantic drama where her boyfriend does this to propose differently.

9. Plot:

You are walking back home. You look for a woman you meet every day. She isn't there today to smile at you from the balcony. A week later, you really want to know where she has gone. You knock the doors of the house. An old woman opens the door and smiles at you the same way. You ask her about the young girl. She takes you in and makes you sit on the couch. She vanishes into a room and this young girl emerges out of the same room.

Development

a.   This old woman might possess a potion that will turn her into a young woman.

b.   There can be a young woman inside and you can develop the story into a romance story.

c.   Both of them, the girl and the old woman, are spirits making your story into a horror story.

d.   Or you can make the girl take him into that room. This room can be a huge, abandoned palace but from outside looks like a single room. Something like Narnia.

10. Plot:

You receive a book in a post. The cover has your photograph and the title of the book is your name.

Development

a. You might make yourself a writer and this could be your autobiography. Then you can start telling people about each chapter of the book.

b. This can be a book written about you by someone. Finding who that writer is can become your book.

c. As you read it you realize it has every important happening of your life written. It also has future dates. You quickly turn to the current date, read it and you find that 'you will receive a book in post that will change your life altogether.' Later after a few days, you realize the book has your fate written. Everything happens according to the book.

11. Plot:

He hears someone knock his door. He rushes to open it assuming it's his girlfriend. He finds no one at the door but a parcel lying at the door steps. The parcel has a note on top of it.

Development

a. You can turn this story into anything depending on what's written on the note.

i. For example, if the note says this has money and you need to do according to what I tell you over the call, this can be an illegal transaction for some illegal work.

ii. If it says, this parcel has the head of your friend. This can become a revenge drama.

iii. If the note reads someone else's address but out of curiosity if he opens it to find so much money, this story can turn into a chase novel.

b. This parcel can be from his girlfriend. She wants to break up with him and has returned everything she has that reminds her of him.

c. The parcel can be an Amazon delivery of anything, even a condom. You can turn it into erotica.

12. Plot:

One morning, you receive a book that you had ordered. Reading it you find that the entire story was yours; from the manuscript, you had submitted to a publishing house.

Development

a. This can become a legal thriller. You file a complaint and fight for your rights. How you win the case becomes the story.

b. Make it mere coincidence. You write another book and that again becomes a book by someone else. Why is this happening?

i. You are a spirit of a writer who died years ago before publishing even one of his work. So you haunt people make them write stories but you don't realize that you have haunted them once you leave them after the book, is written.

ii. You are not aware that you are writing it on your blog. You assume that it's a private space but give out stories as you are ignorant about the internet.

13. **Plot:**

You are sitting in the beach shore with a pen and a paper, wanting to start writing a book. Someone runs to you, hands over a paper and runs into the ocean. A few minutes later this person vanishes into the sea.

Development

a. The paper the person handed over reads,

i. 'This is my story, develop it into a book. This is my last wish.'

ii. 'You are the reason I am dying today.'

iii. 'Send this letter to the address at the backside.' And the address in the back side of the paper is half written. You spend your life finding who this person is and why she wanted the letter to reach the address. You meet different kinds of people in your attempt to find the address. At last, you find that it's your address she wanted the letter to reach. A sequel can be developed on why she wanted to deliver the letter to him and who she was to him.

14. **Plot:**

You are watching the TV Show 'Honey I shrunk the kids'. The laser tip turns to you and the laser hits you. You shrink.

Development

a. This can be made into a comedy script. By making the guy trying to make people notice him, trying to rob a bank and is not even able to move a coin.

b. This can be made into an emotional roller coaster by writing about how hard it was for him to make his girlfriend look at him, feed him till he regains his original size.

15. Plot:

You wake up to find that your blog has been wiped. There is not a single post and you don't have a backup. You had been writing with a pen name and no one knows that it was you. Now you have lost your virtual identity.

16. Plot:

You clean your garage to find a bag full of your old diaries. You had stopped writing diaries two years ago. You decide to read them all.

Development

a. You can make yourself an amnesiac. You have lived with wiped out memory for two long years trusting what people told you. Now it's time to find the truth. (This is a hit formula. Several Amnesiac stories have become hits and there is so much scope. My first book, Just you, me and a secret, was based on similar grounds and I loved writing it.)

b. You are a normal person. AS you read you find that some lines have been added to your diaries changing the entire context of each happening in your life.

i. These changes are in a different handwriting and you are sure you have not written it. Who has written these lines and for what?

ii. These changes or inclusions are made with your handwriting. It gives you a picture that you have written it. But most of it doesn't have an effect in your current life and feels so distant. For instance, the diary entry says you bought a car but in reality, you can't afford a car. Towards the end, you discover that this diary is from yourself but from a parallel universe. You connect to the other "YOU".

17. Plot:

King of a huge empire dies and the prince becomes the king. Later the queen discovers that when she had given birth there was a floor and due to the mess in the country, her maid was also let to give birth to her kid in the same room. The kids were interchanged without the queen knowledge. Now, what will she do? The king is a maid's son. Her real son is a soldier. Letting this news out will create chaos in the country as the kingdom was ruled by a maid's son so long.

Development

a. The kids were interchanged by the maid on purpose. Why?

b.   The king was the biological father of the maid's son too.

c.   The interchange was accidental and how the queen cleverly makes her own son the king of the country is the story.

18.   Plot:
A girl is pinned to a bed, naked. She is struggling to get rid of the handcuffs that locks her to the bed. She is being filmed.

Development

a.   Porn shoot. The life of a porn star.

b.   The girl has been kidnapped and how a superhero saves such girls.

c.   The girl is raped, killed and thrown away in the sea shore. Her boyfriend finds the gang that's involved in woman trafficking and burns them to ashes.

d.   Her father finds her before she is sold. This is like the movie 'Taken'. But you can give it a different side so that it doesn't exactly be like Taken.

19.   Plot:
Skeleton burst out of the ground after a storm unearths a huge tree.

Development

a. A story that involved archeology in which they find when the human of this skeleton had lived. Uncovering mysteries about a particular period in history. This requires a lot of research.

b. This can again be developed into horror. A story around the talking skeleton blown out of the ground.

20. **Plot:**

A dead skeleton is unearthed based on a tip off cops receive. It's found that this skeleton was half burnt before being buried. It's later found that it's the sister of an industrialist.

Development

a. Who killed the girl? The sister? Why?

b. The girl is not the sister but the daughter of this industrialist. She has told the world a big fat lie that the victim was her sister. Now, who killed the girl and why?

More such twists can be brought about in this story. This is a real case in India. Check out the murder mystery of Sheena Bora to get more ideas on this plot.

21. **Plot:**

You think about something and the stranger next to you responds to it as if he heard you speak that. Later, you realize that your ability to think has been lost and all you can do is voice it out assuming that you are thinking about it.

22. **Plot:**

You gain the power to listen to what other people think.

23. Plot:

You gain the power to become invisible. (Okay, this one is a well-known prompt but the more unique your story is the more you sell.) What do you do when no one can see you?

Development

a. Scope for erotica, right?

b. You steal a bank, but money is visible. So what will you steal or how will you steal to become rich? You can add some more spice by having some restrictions on being invisible like you become visible if you get angry or if you laugh.

24. Plot:

You gain the power to talk to animals.

Development

a. One such animal had seen a murder and tells you everything about it.

b. One animal tells you how badly a zoo treats animals. You save the rest of them from that Zoo. Bring the cruelty to light

c. You learn about how much your ex-wife loved you from your pet and fall in love with her once again.

25. Plot:

You have been married for ten years. You suddenly realize that your husband was never in love with you. It was always you who were crazy about him. There is this cute guy who likes you. What will you do?

26. Plot:

You are happily married to a guy, who loved you like crazy. This was after a heartbreak you had from your previous relationship which was on for quite some time. Then you bump into your ex-boyfriend, you were head over heels in love with. Your battle between the love for your husband, who takes care of you so well and your ex-boyfriend whom you really loved is the story.

Development

a.   Love, marriage, ex-boyfriend is enough to twist in itself. So I am not writing ways to branch it out.

27. Plot:

You are a book. Someone reads you and you talk along with them as they read. So the book becomes the narrator.

28. Plot:

You are in the middle of an abandoned desert looking for water. You have traveled a long way in search of water and it's been quite a while since you had last few drops.

Development

a.   How you landed up there can be a good story line.

b. Why you are there in the desert can be another story line. There should be a solid reason for you to take the hardship.

c. What you do in the desert and your hunt for water can become another story. My personal preference is this one but writing this is difficult. One man abandoned desert and you have to write a book out of it. Like the life of pi.

d. You can write all the above into series of books.

29. Plot:

You are in a marathon with hundreds of people. You look at a girl who runs next to you. She falls down all of a sudden without any reason. A few steps ahead you establish eye contact with another guy and he falls down too. You realize that looking into your eyes makes them faint.

Development

a. You are an amazing sport. You try your best not to establish eye contact with anyone.

b. You are an athlete and if this news spreads you will be banned from running. You had already had the dream to win gold for your country in Olympics.

c. You are desperate to win. You try and make everyone look at your eyes. How did you gain the power can run along with the marathon. Go back and forth with the timeline so that the entire book travels in the marathon's timeline, in reality, but flashes back so that the story is written in between.

30. Plot:

You see a celebrity being shot to death by a group. You run to the cops and report the murder. They then find that the celebrity you say is dead is all alive.

Development

a. The guy, who they think is the celebrity, can be a look-a-like and this can be a master plan to loot his money and enjoy his fame. Maybe a twin brother.

b. All that you saw was just a dream and you confused it with reality. After a few days, you read a news piece that the same celebrity was shot to death the same way.

i. Police take you into custody as you told them about this. They find your dream story not so sensible and accuse you of the crime.

ii. With the details from the dream, you help the cops find the killer.

31. Plot:

He proposed marriage to her and waited for her response. She agreed to it but said she was sure she would break up with him in a year.

32. Plot:

She was neatly dressed. She was heading to the table he said he had booked a table in an email. It was her first blind date. She was not happy with her husband. Yes, she was cheating on him.

Development

a. Her husband is the guy who has booked the table. They both had not revealed the identity to each other and had enrolled in a dating website with fake names.

b. She falls in love with the guy who she meets. She tries to get out of her marriage.

33. Plot:

She wanted to become a singer but could not afford to quit her job and start practicing. She was a single mom.

34. Plot:

A gun was pointed at his forehead. He smiled. The trigger was pulled. The police couldn't arrest the killer.

Development

a. Could be because it was a suicide. Finding why the guy committed suicide can become a story.

b. Because the killer ran. You can make him leave some clues. Finding the killer can be the plot.

c.   You can make it a dream and start from there. Why did he even get this dream?

35.   Plot:

Your train stops, abruptly, somewhere between two stations. You see a group of weirdly dressed people standing on either side of the train. A few of the shirtless men, who are bleeding from all over the body, bang on the glass covered window, leaving stains of their blood on it. Who are these men? Who has beaten them mercilessly? Who is the group of people witnessing this unkind act? Why has the train stopped at this weird place? Answering these questions will lead you to write a story.

36.   Plot:

You get back home to find your dog bark at you like you were a stranger.

Development

a.   You are dead and you don't realize that. The dog senses the presence of a spirit. Develop the story from there.

b.   You have forgotten your past. You assume that's your house and your dog, but you are wrong.

37.   Plot:

You are stuck in a dark tunnel that you entered with so much joy assuming it to be something else. After you ran for a while, you realize that the tunnel was dark till how far you could see. You have come a long way. You are not sure if going back was closer or the exit at the other end was closer.

Development

a. Make it a dream. This can be a story about a woman stuck in a marriage she doesn't like. She has no way out.

b. Make it real. You are stuck in a real dark tunnel and your journey through it is the story.

c. Make it like the maze runner. You run and then find so many others. You guys realize that it's a game later.

38. Plot:

They looked at each other for the first time. Their lips curved into a smile almost instantly.

Development

a. They were coolies of underground dons. They were there to exchange something that was illegal. There was some code that made them recognize the other and smiling was part of the plan.

b. They had been chatting on facebook for a long time. They had fallen in love with each other. But that was the first time they met.

39. Plot:

You are a pet and you hate your owner. Your struggle to escape that house.

Development

a. You can make this house filled with pets and this one animal tries to relieve them all.

b. It can be a battle to get back home for that pet; to get back to its family.

40. Plot:

That night he saw a missed call from his dead girlfriend's mobile.

Development

a. His girlfriend died to hang herself all of a sudden a few months ago. She had called to tell him it wasn't suicide but murder. This can give you a lead to a horror story.

b. It can become a mystery. The guy who has the mobile phone has something to do with her death. Finding him is the crux of the story.

41. Plot:

You try to move, but you realize you are frozen. Later you move but not according to your will.

Development

a. You are a shadow of a person. How you became that shadow and how you become a human again is the story.

b. You are a toy of a kid and this story can become a kids books.

c. You are a remote human or a robot. How the robots finally become just like humans and create a new world can be a branch to this story.

42. Plot:

A cook decides to start a restaurant. Love. Hate. Betrayal. This plot has so much potential.

43. Plot:

A five-year-old starts to write books and they all become best sellers.

Development

a. The child was haunted by a writer's ghost. The story of the writer and how he died before his first book was published can become a story.

b. Someone using the kid's name to publish and why? Is there an organized crime behind all of these? The answers to these can make a story.

44. Plot:

Every day your facebook status gets updated automatically. Initially, you think someone hacked your account and change the password. Later you realize this is happening every day and the statuses are like the prediction of your day. No one else is able to see it but you.

Development

a. A story about how a mishap is posted and you try your best making it not happen.

b. A story about finding that person who is dictating your life through facebook statuses.

45. Plot:

A famous dancer meets with an accident. He is advised by the doctor not to dance anymore.

Development

a. A Motivational story of how he then becomes a dance trainer and comes up in life.

b. An emotional story that revolves around his struggle. How the world forgets successful people after they have a downfall.

46. Plot:

You wake up and look into the mirror to see a stranger staring at you.

Development

a. Could be a horror story.

b. Turn it into a story of an amnesiac.

47. Plot:

You realize that time moves according to your breath. If you want to freeze a second just hold your breath. And if you want time to move faster breathe faster. What will you do? When will you freeze the moment?

Development

a. You can make it something like the movie click. You govern the movement of time. And one day you don't want time to move. You keep holding your breath and you die.

48. Plot:

You buy a book from a second-hand bookstore. After you come back home you find a note written in one of the pages.

Development

a. Make it a thriller. Every chapter end's with a note that was written with pen and not printed. There is a mystery that you can make the protagonist find.

b. A beautiful love story can evolve from here. She can find the guy who had written those beautiful poetic lines after each chapter. Falls in love with him.

49. Plot:

She has the power to foresee things. She has the power to find out if you lied to her.

Development

a. A relationship that she gets in. The pain she goes through each time she listens to dear ones though she knows that they are lying to her.

b. She becomes a part of the FBI.

c. She is kidnapped by a greedy gangster to know what will happen to him and detect when people lied to him. She secretly works for him. One day, her dad sits in the detection chair. He lies. Will she reveal it? What did he lie about? Why was he there? You can add more twists by making her face turn red if she ever lied. So how she comes out of this situation will be a bit challenging to write and very interesting to read.

50. Plot:

A treasure map accidentally lands in your mailbox. What will you do?

Development

a. You can use this to develop it into different genres based on what that treasure is.

51. Plot:

You win a dinner date with your favorite celebrity through a TV Show. During the date, she tells you a secret about herself. Next day she is found dead in her apartment mysteriously.

52. Plot:

You work at a jewelry shop. A group of men with their faces covered barge into the shop with guns.

Development

a. How will you save yourself? An entire book just about that day. Very challenging but if written, this will pan out into an amazing story.

b. How will you save the jewels? Can become a crime thriller.

c. What if you are a part of the gang and you got yourself employed there just for this day.

53. Plot:
As his boss neared him, he deleted several emails from her.

54. Plot:
As his wife came out of the kitchen, he disconnected the phone.

Development

a. Extramarital affair.

b. Illegal business

c. Call regarding wife's extramarital affair.

d. Planning for a surprise birthday party for the wife.

55. Plot:
You meet yourself as a third person.

Development

a. You can see yourself as a third person when you are haunted. This becomes a horror story.

b. This can happen when you time travel. A good scope for science fiction.

c.   This can happen when you have the power to look at you from outside. (Fantasy)

d.   When you can foresee future. This has a good scope for a thriller story. You can foresee yourself harming someone and try hard not to do anything that you think would lead to it.

56. Plot:

You look into the mirror and after a while, your reflection walks out of the mirror.

Development

a.   Horror: Easier to make this a horror story by calling the reflection that walked out as a spirit.

b.   Philosophy: It becomes a philosophical story when you make the reflection walk with you all the time, guiding you about what's good and what's not.

c.   Thriller: When the girl commits suicide and later after several investigation it's found that she was mentally unstable. This can be found from a video or diary she wrote before her death.

57. Plot:

You break up with someone and run away from home. How do you start a new life?

Development

a. The story can be completely about how the girl enjoys her newly found independence.

b. The story can be about how she regrets and the incidents that reminds her of him. She can get back to him at the end of the book, making it a happy ending story.

58. Plot:

You wake up to find that you have special powers. You will be able to tune into an invisible camera placed at every house, in every room of theirs.

Development

a. This has high potential to become an erotica.

b. Detective. Crime thriller. This prompt can be developed into a detective story where the detective possesses this power. To make it interesting, we can add some strange restrictions to this like he will be able to use this power only if he is a certain meter away. Or even crazier like only when he wears nothing or is alone in a closed room. Mom and dad are getting divorced. Robert, the kid, decides to live alone in a hostel. How Robert brings together mom and dad makes a story. How he makes them fall in love again.

59. Plot:

You are house arrested along with your family by a group of gunmen. They don't let you move and escort you even to use the washroom. You have no way to escape with their eyes open.

60. Plot:

Every day, after a certain hour of the day you lose the power to hear. But if this is known to your employer your employment will be at stake.

Development

a. You can have a son, little one, and single dad. The pursuit of happiness can be a reference. But make it different.

b. Humor is something we didn't cover much in this prompt book. This can be handled as a humor script.

61. Plot:

The teacher enters into a class. Suddenly, a student from the last row screams. The teacher walks to the student as the student shivers. The student points under the desk.

Development:

1. There is a guy fully drenched with blood and a knife in his hand. His face is covered. He threatens to kill the kid if the teacher doesn't let him hide there for a few hours.

    a. 'Who is this guy? Why was he there?' this can be made into a story.

b. 'How does the teacher save the kids? How does she intelligently handles him and at the same time call the cop to inform about this guy.

c. The story of the teacher and how this incident changes her life altogether.

2. There is a bag full of money.

   a. Who dropped it there? Why was it dropped there? Is the person still around? Should she inform the cops about it?

   b. The teacher being a part of the robbery of a bank and making her use the school as a hideout. What does she do with the classroom full of children who have found her secret? Who will save these kids from the teacher?

   c. The teacher greedily picks up the bag and hides it somewhere. She plans to run away with it. She is being chased by the group that hid the bag in the school. Will she escape from these smugglers? Will she get away with the money? Who will save her from this?

62. Plot:

A mom is separated from her child as the child's dad has a better financial support to take care of the kid. Post the divorce, the mom tries her best to be financially stable in order to get back the kid.

Development:

1. The kid grows up without knowing who his mom is. The mom tries to meet the kid outside the house but fails to make the kid trust her. She, then, decides to become the teacher of the school the kid is put in. She becomes the kid's favorite teacher. Will the kid accept her as the mom? Will the dad allow the kid to continue in the same school the next year knowing that the mom is there?

2. The kid grows not knowing who her mom is and why her parents were separated. The teacher helps the kid find her mother.

3. The teacher falls in love with the kid's dad. The kids battle to bring her mom and dad together, keeping the teacher away from her dad. This can be developed into a comedy story if the kid's perspective is major. Else, this can be developed into romance if the teacher's or dad's perspective is major.

63. Plot:

There is an accident that occurs inside prison and a prisoner loses his memory.

Development:

1. Social drama can be made with this Plot. One can write a story around how the punishment of imprisonment goes waste because of the memory loss of the prisoner.

2. The prisoner is a terrorist and was the only lead to reach a majorly active group of militants. He has lost his memory. Now, how will the cops find the group with him?
   i. The cops could make him the weapon and bring the group out. They can tell him he is an actor and record some videos which will indirectly make the group come out on its own.

   ii. The group of terrorists can take this guy back and later discover that he has forgotten everything.

   iii. The terrorist could have been a cop who was in an undercover operation. The cops try to make him understand this, but the group of terrorists takes him under their custody. Shows him the photographs and proofs that he was a part of their group. How will the cops recover this guy? Will the terrorists find that he was on an undercover operation and kill?

64. Plot:

A prisoner tries to escape the prison. He, religiously, works on to find the floor plan of the prison. Every day he walks a different path and later marks it down in his blueprint paper. One fine day, when he has the entire floor plan, he decides to run away. If he missed that night, he must wait for another one year for the same day.

Development:

1. His plan is lost. He doesn't know it by heart. He keeps searching, but all his efforts to locate the map goes in vain. The next morning he finds it in his pocket, the only place he had missed searching. This can be developed into a humorous story.

2. He runs away. The cop, who is the protagonist, finds this plan and traces behind the escaped prisoner. The intelligent mind games between the escaped prisoner and the cop is the story.

65. Plot:

You plan a birthday party. Everyone comes and there is a stranger who enters the party hall. Just to avoid the awkward moment you don't ask him who he is. He leaves after handing over a gift to you.

Development:

1. You are a cop and you get too curious to know what's in there. But you are suspicious and hence you don't want to open it in the party place. At the same time you leaving the party hall just with that one wrapped gift will create a chaos and tension at the party place. This becomes a thriller.

2. You are a female. The guy looked so smart and his smile was so compelling for you to open the gift right away, taking it to a corner. It's a love proposal. This can be developed into a romance story.

3. The gift contains a huge sum of money. There is a note stating that you should finish off the money within a month if not you will be killed. You try to trace the person leaving the money to you and the reason behind this. Meanwhile you also get scared and start spending money. Thriller again but has the potential to make it into a political thriller or a financial thriller.

66. Plot:

Your protagonist are in love with someone but her wedding is fixed with someone else.

Development:

1. She is an amnesiac. The guy her marriage is fixed with is someone she was in love with before she lost her memory. A romantic suspense can be woven. My debut novel _Just you me and a secret_ was written from this Plot.

2. Just after her engagement she fell out of love with the guy. Now after making arrangements for her wedding she realizes that she is in love with someone else. It has good scope to be turned into a romance story.

3. She loves a guy but agrees for a wedding with a rich guy assuming that's right for her life. How does she battle with her actual feelings and the one she is masking? This again is a romance story.

67. Plot:

Your protagonist doesn't get her periods. She checks with a doctor casually and get shocked when she discovers that she is pregnant.

Developments:

1. She went to a pub for the first time a month or so ago and got drunk. She went with two of her colleagues. She has no idea who has done this to her. She tries to find out with clues and cctv footage. This can become a thriller.

2. This Plot has a good scope to be turned into an erotica or drama. You can make her a prostitute. She has no clue which intercourse has led to pregnancy. Now her living that's based on her earning through sex would be cut off. What will she do to the pregnancy? Abort it?

   a. Struggle of managing the pimps and hiding the pregnancy till she aborts. The pain of every prostitute who sleeps with people for day to day needs can be brought out.

   b. She decides to bring up the baby in the brother. The baby can grow up into a strong woman who achieves something in life. The life of kids in brothels can be written into a beautiful book that can even be worth the awards.

3. She can be a model. She must have signed a contract to not become pregnant. The painful lives of models can be brought out. How they vomit the minute after they eat. How they have to always dress well.

4. This can again be made into an erotica by making her a wife of a rich businessman who has gone on a business trip three months ago. She has an extra marital affair with her driver.

68. Plot:
You fall in love with your best friend's girlfriend. You know for a fact that she likes you. You don't want to hurt your friend.

Developments:

1. The struggle that you go through to contain your love for her just not to hurt your friends can be brought out into a beautiful romance fiction.

2. You guys have an undercurrent romance without your friend's knowledge. The day he discovers this he breaks up with her and stops interacting with you. Out of guilt you stop talking to her. The three of you take a different route only to meet each other at a friend's wedding and start talking again. This time the two of you try to impress her. The story of the three can be made into a romance story.

69. Plot:
You read a book and the characters come alive one after the other. They are real people and behave exactly like it's mentioned in the book. Later you realize that the protagonist of the book is you and you are reading your future.

Developments:

1. You read it as fast as possible. There is an accident that's described in the book. You take a pen and strike it off. The pen strike on the page of the book prevents the accident from happening. You keep preventing things from happening. It's good for a while until something else that's worse happens. At this point you discover that if you write something in the book you are able to rewrite your future. How you use the book becomes a fantasy story.

2. According to the book you will be haunted by a ghost. You try all you can to prevent that scenario from happening. You avoid taking that route as mentioned in the book. The content in the book starts getting altered based on the changes you make. But the part where the ghost haunts you still remains the same. How you tackle the ghost can be woven into a horror story.

3. You become a fortune teller. You start amazing people with the book that you have. You become famous and rich. On a very important day when the president of US wants to meet you to know about America's future you lose the book. How do you manage?! This has a lot of potential to become a humour story.

70. Plot:

You are stuck in an island. The island map is in your hand. Slowly you discover that each gate of the island is a puzzle that you need to solve in order to escape from there.

Developments:

1. You can make it fantasy by making the puzzles dreamy.

2. You can make it an historic fiction by making the setting based on what knowledge you acquire about a particular period.

3. You can even make it a video game that a person is struck in. To make the person come out the other person playing the game must win the game.

71. Plot:

A beautiful girl joins a rich school. She is beautiful but poor. The girls there humiliate her for the clothes she wears and the bag she brings. A rich guy from the school falls in love with her. He breaks up before he proposes this poor girl. The news travels to his mom who owns the school.

Developments:

1. The next morning she is found dead. Who killed her? This can become a thriller. You can make the ex, his mom and a few others as suspects.

2. His mom dismisses her from school. She gets angry with him for being the reason for her exit from the school. How he makes her nod a yes and how he brings her back to the school becomes the story. This can be a nice young adult romance.

3. She is a rich girl who has accepted a challenge from her dad to live like a girl with no money. She wants to be on her own. She dislikes him for being so dependent on his parent's wealth. How she changes his mind set and the mindset of the rest of the students. This makes a perfect drama.

72. Plot:

You receive a phone call in the middle of the night. A girl asks you to sing a song. You disconnect the line and turn back to see a girl standing, scarily dressed just behind you. She asks you to sing and has the same voice as in the phone call.

Developments:

1. She is the girl who lived in the house you just occupied before you. She committed suicide in the same spot where you have placed your phone. The reason for her suicide and how she takes revenge on people who troubled her when she was alive with your help becomes a horror story.

2. It's your birthday and this is a trick your girlfriend is playing with you. But out of fear you lose your ability to speak. She decides to stay with you forever as your voice. Turns into a romance story.

73. Plot:

She packed her bags with tears welling her eyes. She had to make that choice. She had to bear the pain that the choice had given her for a lifetime. Or maybe it will subside as she creates a new world around her, as she moves on with life. But now it was very painful to leave the life she was living. It was a decision she had made after giving it a thought for more than a year.

Developments:

1. She was leaving her home, her husband and her marriage behind. She loved him more but things weren't working out anymore. She wanted to run away, destroy her identity and start a new life. (Romance)
    a. He was an abusive husband and hence she wanted to leave. It pained her to leave as she was scared of the hardships she had to face before creating a new identity for her. She was in pain as she was leaving her identity along with the abusive husband. It wasn't easy for her. (Can be developed into a psychological Thriller.)

    b. She loved her husband but was sure that she wasn't the right one for him. It was because of her that he was not performing well at work. They were colleagues and her success killed him. Her promotion considered over his made him shrink within. He was failing time and again but she was successful always. This created a lot of problems in their marriage and she thought it had to end for the benefit of the two. (Drama)

   c. She had killed her husband out of anger, accidentally. She didn't want to stay back and go behind bars for the rest of her life. She wanted to run away with the money that was there and make it look like she was abducted. (Crime Thriller)

2. She was with her single mom all her life. Suddenly, her mom passed away. Before she could get over the loss a man comes to take her to his home. He says he is her biological dad and had claimed guardianship in the court as she is just fourteen.

   a. The man is really her dad and takes her to a new life. She gets into a new school at the city her dad lives in. How a teenager feels being amidst a group of strangers and how she makes friends. Her first love can be a major part of the story too. (Young- adult romance, coming of age)

   b. The man isn't her dad. All the evidences he showed her was fake. He forces her into prostitution. How she takes revenge and how she escapes out of the brother can become a thriller story. (Thriller)

74. Plot:

You meet a person on road. She tries to save your life and in the process the bus hits her and she dies in your arm. You have no clue who she is but she lost her life to save yours.

Developments:

1. She haunts you as a ghost. She guides you to her parents and you decide you will take care of them taking her place in the family. (Drama)

2. You find out who the girl is to inform her friends and relatives about the accident and her death. As you find more about her past you fall in love with her. That is when her spirit appears in front of you. You guys fall in love with each other but you being a human and she being a spirit living together for long isn't your future for sure. The struggle of loving someone knowing very well that you are not meant to be can be written as a beautiful romance story.

75 Plot:

He over-hears his boss discussing about firing him from the job.

Developments:

1. You device a plan to impress your boss. The story can be entirely set in an office like in the movie "Pursuit of Happiness". What struggles you will go through in your personal life if you are fired can be a major part of the story.

a. This can be written as a family drama. If his loss of job is going to affect the family.

b. This can be made into a beautiful romance story where he struggles to manage his time between his job, that he was going to lose, and his girlfriend. How he struggles for money and keep the news away from her. This also has scope for Humor.

2. You are sure that you will be thrown out of the job very soon. You decide to loot a lot of money in a tricky way so that they don't get to track you as the person behind it anytime soon. Depending on the profession he has taken up you can do your research and make it into a financial thriller.

76. Plot:

You are married to someone who loves you crazily. You like your life the way it is. But deep down it pains when you meet your ex, who is also you colleague. You join your ex on a business trip to a new country.

Developments:

1. Love blooms again. Love is a natural feeling and doesn't know if you are married, unmarried, committed or single. You both naturally and gradually fall in love with each other.

2. You are being threatened by your ex to satisfy his sexual needs. He black mails that he would break your marriage.

77. Plot:
You meet a guy every day at a railway station while going to work place. This happens for months together but the two of you haven't exchanged a word.

Developments:

1. One day you decide to walk up to him to ask his name and the relationship starts there.

2. He stops coming to the railway station after a few months. You go in search of him with the little details you were able to collect from the past few months. The journey that leads you to meet him and finally fall in love is the story.

78. Plot:
A single mom of a teenager meets someone she likes. She starts to date him. Her daughter doesn't like the guy she dates.

Developments:

1. She thinks the only way to start a new life with this man she likes is by convincing her daughter. But her daughter is stubborn. Her daughter doesn't want to live in the same house with her boyfriend. The story is about how the man

wins over the heart of the daughter in order to make his story a success with her mom. This written from mom's perspective.

2. Writing the scenario 1 from the guy's perspective will give the story a different flavor. The story can bring out the struggle of this man. How hurtful it would be to be hated by the girlfriend's kid can be written into a beautiful story. This can also show how much he loves the kid's mom that drives him do crazy things to impress the kid.

79. Plot:

She went on a vacation to an island. It was a very small island with a few islanders. The major income of the islanders was tourism as it had many exotic beaches. She was alone and had booked for a guided tour through an online portal. She never thought she would meet someone she would fall in love with there in the island.

Developments:

1. She falls in love with the guide. How different the two of their lives are but how magical love is to bring them together can be made into a nice story. He is someone who hasn't gone out of the island from birth and she is someone who goes on a vacation to a different country every other year.

2. She is being abducted by a group of people involved in trafficking. The island is known for its night life, pubs and brothels. She is taken to a brother. A writer who wants to

write about the lives of prostitutes visit this place where she is forcefully kept. How he saves her from them and the romance that blooms between them makes a super hit Romantic Suspense story.

80. Plot

He marries his high school sweetheart after dating her for several years. They decide to have a baby and settle down as a family. When she finally got pregnant opinions started to differ. She wasn't able to accompany his to the pubs to drink. She wasn't able to smoke cigarettes with him. She wanted his help for most of her routine works. He did not think about the responsibilities that came along with a baby.

Developments:

1. He decides to leave her forever. She is heartbroken and decides to end her life after putting up her baby for adoption. Little did she know that her prince charming was waiting for her. How a pregnant single woman falls in love with someone and how a man decides to get into a relationship with a pregnant woman is the story.

2. They decide to do all they can to make the marriage work. They create a time table of tasks each of them should do to have a healthy baby. They make adjustments. Finally she gives birth to a beautiful kid. He thinks all the adjustment would end here but that's when they had to plan a timetable

for a lifetime. How a kid changes peoples' lives can be brought out into a nice comical story.

Printed in Great Britain
by Amazon